GO JUL 2012
HD JAN 2016

WK DEC 2016
05Feb24

the science of CATASTROPHE

NATURAL DISASTERS
VIOLENT WEATHER

STEVE PARKER & DAVID WEST

Crabtree Publishing Company
www.crabtreebooks.com

Crabtree Publishing Company
www.crabtreebooks.com

Created and produced by:
David West Children's Books

Project development and concept:
David West Children's Books

Authors: Steve Parker and David West
Editor: Adrianna Morganelli
Proofreader: Crystal Sikkens
Designer: David West
Illustrator: David West
Project coordinator: Kathy Middleton
Production and print coordinator: Katherine Berti
Prepress technician: Katherine Berti

Library and Archives Canada Cataloguing in Publication

Parker, Steve, 1952-
    Natural disasters : violent weather / Steve Parker and David West.

(The science of catastrophe)
Includes index.
Issued also in electronic formats.
ISBN 978-0-7787-7574-4 (bound).--ISBN 978-0-7787-7579-9 (pbk.)

    1. Natural disasters--Juvenile literature. 2. Weather--Juvenile literature.
I. West, David, 1956- II. Title. III. Series: Science of catastrophe

GB5019.P37 2011   j904'.5   C2011-905016-1

Library of Congress Cataloging-in-Publication Data

Parker, Steve, 1952-
  Natural disasters. Violent weather / Steve Parker & David West.
       p. cm. -- (The science of catastrophe)
  Includes index.
  ISBN 978-0-7787-7574-4 (reinforced library binding : alk. paper) -- ISBN 978-0-7787-7579-9 (pbk. : alk. paper) -- ISBN 978-1-4271-8857-1 (electronic pdf) -- ISBN 978-1-4271-9760-3 (electronic html.)
 1. Natural disasters--Juvenile literature. 2. Weather--Juvenile literature. I. West, David, 1956- II. Title. III. Title: Violent weather. IV. Series.

GB5019.P376 2012
904'.5--dc23
                                                                        2011027740

Crabtree Publishing Company
www.crabtreebooks.com   1-800-387-7650

Printed in the U.S.A./112011/JA20111018

Copyright © **2012 CRABTREE PUBLISHING COMPANY**. All rights reserved. No part of this publication may be reproduced, stored in a retrieval system or be transmitted in any form or by any means, electronic, mechanical, photocopying, recording, or otherwise, without the prior written permission of Crabtree Publishing Company.

Published in Canada
Crabtree Publishing
616 Welland Ave.
St. Catharines, Ontario
L2M 5V6

Published in the United States
Crabtree Publishing
PMB 59051
350 Fifth Avenue, 59th Floor
New York, New York 10118

Published in the United Kingdom
Crabtree Publishing
Maritime House
Basin Road North, Hove
BN41 1WR

Published in Australia
Crabtree Publishing
3 Charles Street
Coburg North
VIC 3058

Contents

THUNDERSTORM
One of 2,000 That Rage Worldwide at Any One Time
4

MICROBURST
Martinair Flight 495, Faro, Portugal, 1992
6

HAILSTORM
Guizhou Province, South China, 2001
8

HURRICANE
Katrina, United States, 2005
10

CYCLONE
Tracy, Northern Australia, 1974
12

TORNADO
Super-Outbreak, South & East United States, 2011
14

WATERSPOUT
Sydney, Australia, 2011
16

SUPERSTORM
Storm of the Century, Eastern North America, 1993
18

BLIZZARD
Northwest-Central Iran, 1972
20

MONSOON FLOOD
Pakistan, South Asia, 2010
22

SANDSTORM
Northwest Iraq, 2009
24

HEATWAVE
Western Europe, 2003
26

LIGHTNING AND WILDFIRE
Black Saturday, Victoria State, Australia, 2009
28

Disasters World Map 30

Glossary 31

Index 32

Tall, wide-topped "anvil" clouds, with lightning flickering from the dark base, warn of an approaching thunderstorm. (Artist's depiction)

Thunderstorm

ONE OF 2,000 THAT RAGE WORLDWIDE AT ANY ONE TIME

When warm, damp air rises fast into cooler air, its moisture turns from vapor into raindrops and ice crystals. With the right conditions, soon there is a massive storm with lightning, thunder, and torrents of rain and hail.

THE SCIENCE OF THUNDERSTORMS

Thunderstorms are most common where warmer, moist air collides with cool air from a colder region. As the lighter warm air rises and cools, its invisible water vapor **condenses** into water drops. This process gives out heat and warms the air more. Finally at great height, drops freeze into ice and fall in pockets or downdrafts. These spread at ground level as fierce winds, up to 80 miles per hour (130 kilometers per hour). A cumulonimbus thundercloud may be 15 miles (24 kilometers) high and wide, with 500,000 tons (454,000 metric tons) of water.

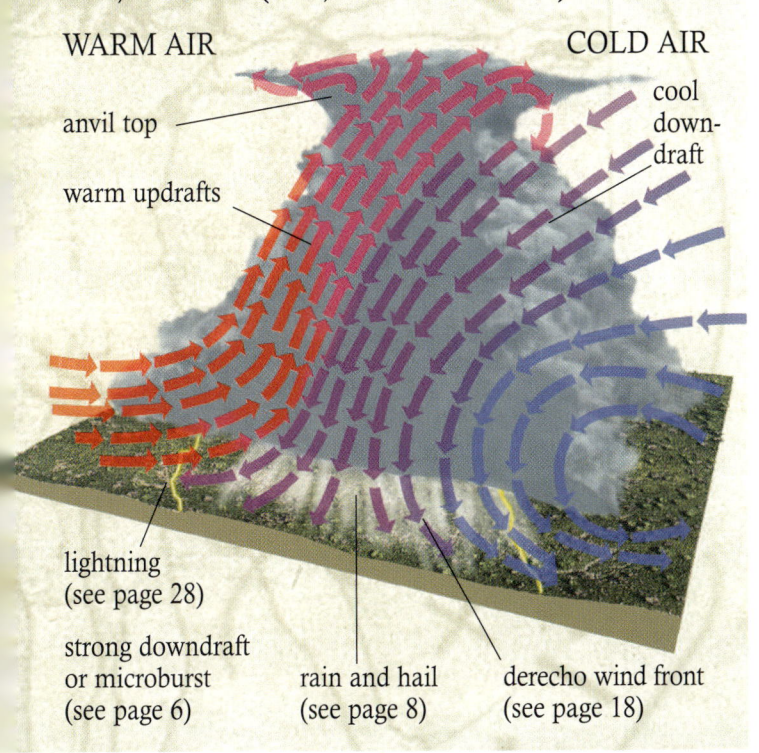

WARM AIR — COLD AIR
- anvil top
- warm updrafts
- cool downdraft
- lightning (see page 28)
- strong downdraft or microburst (see page 6)
- rain and hail (see page 8)
- derecho wind front (see page 18)

It is the end of a hot, dry spell. A cooler mass of air approaches and begins to fight against the warm one. Distant, earth-shaking rumbles of thunder are an early sign that a storm is on its way. Then come towering dark clouds called **cumulonimbus** on the horizon, windy squalls known as **derechos**, perhaps sudden intense microbursts, whirling tornadoes or "twisters," possible heavy hail, and other violent, even deadly features. (All are shown on later pages.) Rain patters lightly then pours down. There is a sudden flash, a boom—and the main storm has arrived.

Thunder is caused by lightning, which is a giant spark or arc of electricity, as described on page 28. The lightning bolt is so hot, tens of thousands of degrees, that it heats the air around it almost instantly. This creates a shock wave that spreads faster than sound, like an aircraft's supersonic boom—the thunder. Light travels about one million times faster than sound. So the time gap between seeing the lightning flash and hearing thunder is 4.5 seconds per mile (3 seconds per kilometer). Near to the lightning, the thunder sounds short and sharp, like a crack. Farther away, its sounds are blown around by wind into deep, rolling rumbles.

Microburst

MARTINAIR FLIGHT 495, FARO, PORTUGAL, 1992

Microbursts are like upside-down, very short-lived mini-tornadoes. They are difficult to forecast—and sometimes deadly. They are suspected of causing several aircraft disasters, including 56 deaths at Faro Airport, Portugal, in 1992.

Microbursts usually come from tall, dark clouds, especially cumulonimbus thunderclouds, as shown on the previous page. Because they last just a few minutes and are so small, less than three miles (four kilometers) across, they are difficult to predict and study. But their fierce winds, as strong as a tornado or twister, produce serious effects. They blow over trees and buildings, pick up cars and people—and make aircraft crash.

On December 21, 1992, the DC-10 of Martinair Flight 495 prepared to land at Faro Airport in southern Portugal. The 327 passengers were mostly Dutch people looking forward to a sunny vacation. The 13 crew had been warned of thunderstorms, and the pilots abandoned the first landing attempt. Second time around, one or possibly two microbursts pushed the plane down too fast. It reached the runway but hit it so hard that one set of wheels and landing gear broke. This tore open a fuel tank in the wing. As the spilling fuel caught fire, the fuselage (main body) of the aircraft broke open and exposed the passengers to the inferno. Besides the 56 dead, more than 100 others were badly burned or injured in the microburst tragedy.

THE SCIENCE OF MICROBURSTS

If rain or hail falls from a large cloud into very dry air, it **evaporates** or turns into water vapor. This process, plus the falling movement of the drops or stones themselves, very rapidly builds up to form an incredibly strong down-current of air. As it reaches the ground, it is pushed outward in a spoke-like pattern. The straight-line winds may reach speeds of 150 miles per hour (240 kilometers per hour).

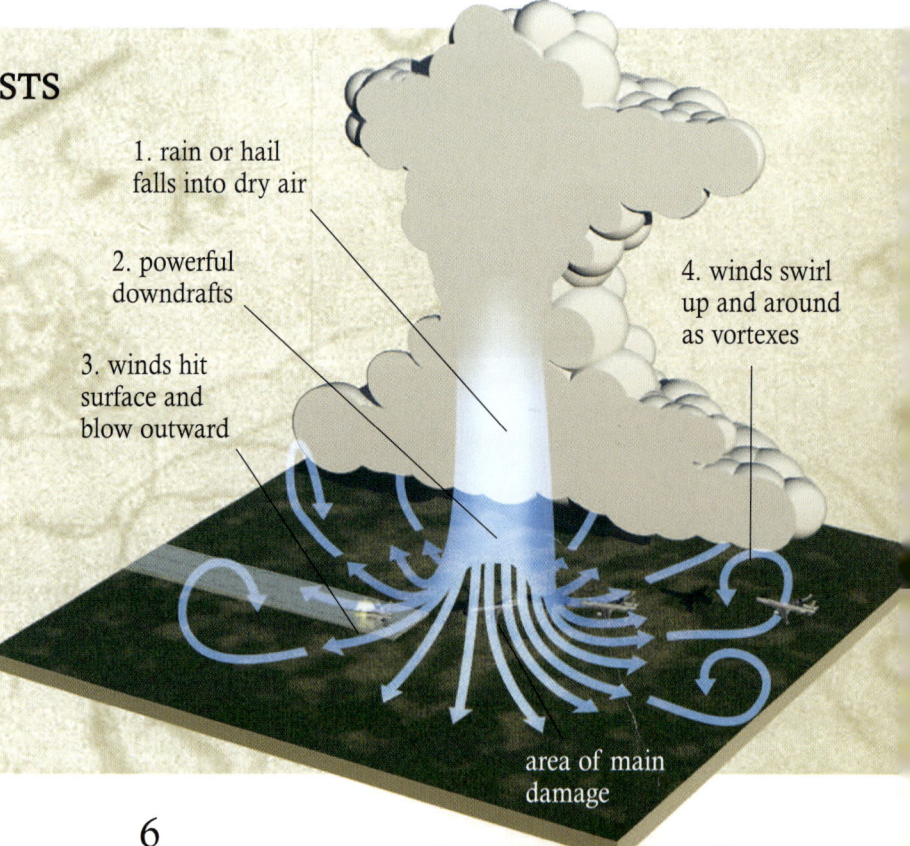

1. rain or hail falls into dry air
2. powerful downdrafts
3. winds hit surface and blow outward
4. winds swirl up and around as vortexes

area of main damage

Martinair's McDonnell Douglas DC-10 fights against the microburst's extreme downdraft as it approaches Faro Airport. (Artist's depiction)

Hailstorm

GUIZHOU PROVINCE, SOUTH CHINA, 2001

A minor shower of hailstones is interesting to watch, but little more. A severe hailstorm can smash windows, cave in buildings and vehicle roofs, take out electrical power lines, and cause serious injury, or even death.

Like microbursts, hailstorms are usually the result of an especially big, tall thundercloud (see previous pages). Inside are updrafts fed by warm air, plus water vapor that condenses into liquid water, giving out more heat. There are also downdrafts of sinking high-altitude air, plus ice or water that evaporates and takes in heat. Drops are caught in a cycle as they rise, freeze into ice, fall, gather water on their outside, rise, and freeze again, and so on. This builds multi-layered balls of ice—hailstones. Eventually these are too heavy to be carried by an updraft, and they fall as a hailstorm.

The smallest hailstones are about 0.2 inches (0.5 centimeters) across. Severe storms produce giants more than eight inches (20 centimeters) wide, weighing almost two pounds (nearly one kilogram). In 2001, China's southern province of Guizhou suffered a series of severe hailstorms. More than 300 stones, some almost two inches (five centimeters) across, fell on each square yard (square meter) of land. Twenty people died, along with 50 farm animals. The storms smashed 5,000 dwellings, broke car windows and dented their roofs, and flattened 300 square miles (777 square kilometers) of crops.

THE SCIENCE OF HAILSTORMS

Thunderstorm formation is shown on page 5. Hailstones grow in very tall thunderclouds where the upper portion has air well below freezing point, 32 degrees Fahrenheit (0 degrees Celsius). As ice particles fall, water collects on them. They are blown up, and the water freezes as an ice layer. The cycle happens several times, growing stones that become so heavy they fall to the ground.

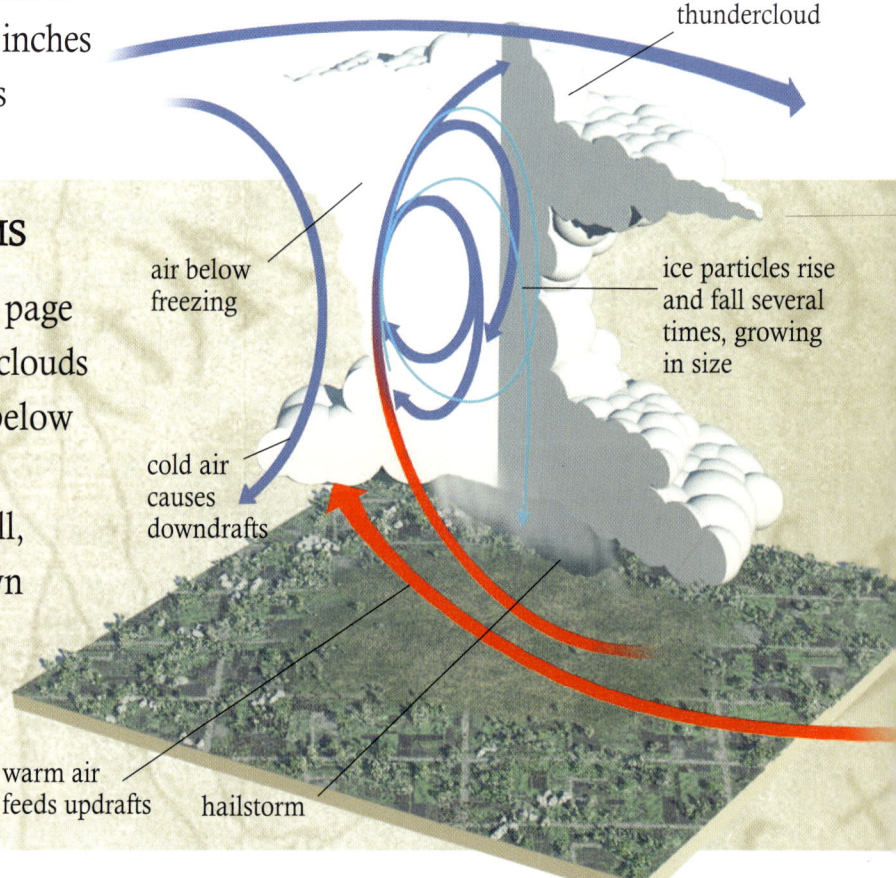

Huge hailstones hammer down in Guiyang, the capital of Guizhou Province. (Artist's depiction)

THE SCIENCE OF HAIL

Hailstones grow by a layer about 1/25th of an inch (one millimeter) thick with each up-and-down trip inside the thundercloud.

- many layers of clear or frosted-looking ice inside the stone
- central nucleus such as dust particle

9

Hurricane
KATRINA, UNITED STATES, 2005

Every year, hurricanes wreak havoc in the West Atlantic, Caribbean, and Gulf of Mexico. Katrina was Number Six for strength, Three for Americans dead, and One for costs.

Atlantic hurricanes, Pacific typhoons, and southern cyclones are some of the biggest, most violent weather on our planet. They are all forms of **tropical cyclones**, with swirling high winds and torrential rains (see next page). The Atlantic produces an average of five to ten full-scale hurricanes each year, peaking around late summer and early fall. The 2005 season was the worst recorded, with 15 named hurricanes. Katrina met land over Florida in the last week of August, and headed west as the weakest kind of hurricane, Category 1. It moved on southwest, leading to hopes it would blow out in the Gulf of Mexico. But it veered around northward and strengthened hugely to Category 5, with winds of 170 miles per hour (280 kilometers per hour).

Reducing to Category 3, Katrina hit the Mississippi River Delta on August 29, and roared onward, north over the Breton Sound, to make landfall a third time near the Louisiana-Mississippi state line. Now some 250 miles (400 kilometers) across, its path left enormous areas almost wiped flat. Along the Gulf Coast, the high water of the storm surge burst through sea walls and levees to flood towns, roads, rail, and farms inland. New Orleans was devastated, with water covering four-fifths of the city. More than 1,800 died in the hurricane itself and the following floods. Katrina continued north, gradually fading to small tail-end squalls that reached as far as the Great Lakes on August 31.

Katrina blasts ashore onto the U.S. Gulf Coast, beginning its vast trail of destruction. (Artist's depiction)

THE SCIENCE OF HURRICANES

A hurricane has ring-like or spiraling fierce rainstorms with a calm center, the eye. It begins in a similar way to a thunderstorm, but over warm ocean water (see pages 5 and 12). This water must be at least 80 degrees Fahrenheit (27 degrees Celsius) to a depth of 160 feet (49 meters), to provide the huge energy input and water vapor. Wind speeds for a Category 1 hurricane are over 74 miles per hour (119 kilometers per hour). An average-sized hurricane is about 300 miles (480 kilometers) across.

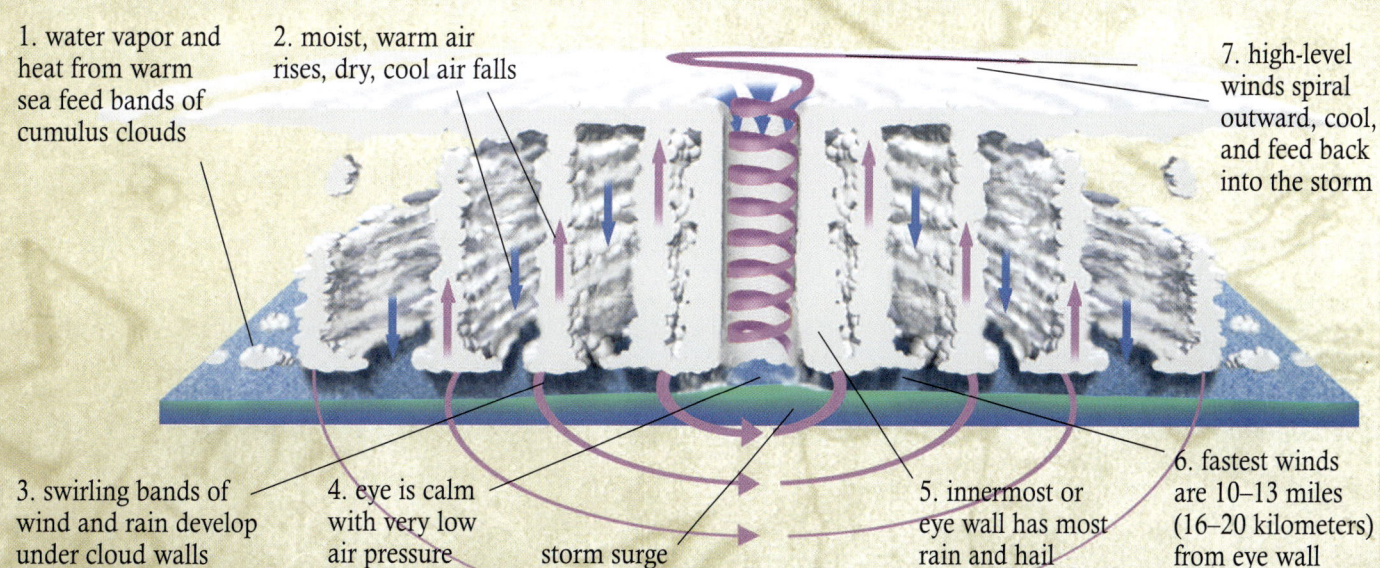

1. water vapor and heat from warm sea feed bands of cumulus clouds
2. moist, warm air rises, dry, cool air falls
3. swirling bands of wind and rain develop under cloud walls
4. eye is calm with very low air pressure
5. innermost or eye wall has most rain and hail
6. fastest winds are 10–13 miles (16–20 kilometers) from eye wall
7. high-level winds spiral outward, cool, and feed back into the storm

storm surge

THE SCIENCE OF CYCLONE FORMATION

As shown on the previous page, the Sun's heat warms the ocean surface so much that moist air rises, then cools at a certain height, and condenses into rain. The rising air pulls in cooler air from around, which also heats and rises, and so on. Gradually separate storms combine as one swirling mass which may be a hurricane, typhoon, or simply "cyclone."

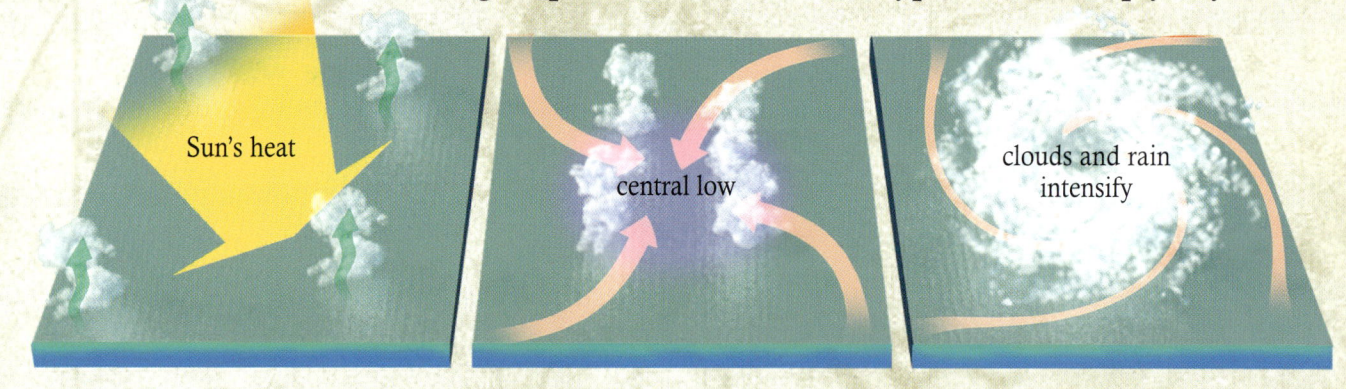

1. The Sun heats up the ocean's surface, creating rainstorms.

2. The rising air creates low pressure, drawing in more storms and winds.

3. The winds rotate due to Coriolis and other forces, and a cyclone forms.

Cyclone
TRACY, NORTHERN AUSTRALIA, 1974

Cyclones, also called **depressions** or lows, are areas where air swirls around and also gradually moves inward, like a spiral. The direction they rotate in depends on whether they are north or south of the Equator. In 1974, Cyclone Tracy ripped apart the city of Darwin, in northern Australia.

Hurricanes (see previous page) are types of tropical cyclones. These storms, with intense low air pressure at the center, are known simply as "cyclones" in some regions, such as around the Indian Ocean and Australia. South of the equator, their winds spiral clockwise. To the north, they go counterclockwise, due to Earth's rotation and the **Coriolis Effect**.

On December 24, 1974, people in Darwin, the capital of Australia's Northern Territories, were ready to celebrate Christmas. But then Cyclone Tracy arrived. It was small, hardly less than 100 miles (160 kilometers) across. But its winds of 150 miles per hour (240 kilometers per hour) flattened two-thirds of Darwin's buildings. In just a few hours, 71 people were dead, and 40,000—three-quarters of the city-dwellers—were homeless.

Away from the tropics are **extratropical cyclones** (see page 18). They may be thousands of miles (kilometers) wide, move as fast as 1,000 miles (1,600 kilometers) each day, last for a week or more, and bring unsettled weather, winds, clouds, and rain.

THE SCIENCE OF THE CORIOLIS EFFECT

The Coriolis Effect is due to Earth's shape and rotation. It makes moving objects north of the equator angle or deflect to the right, and to the left if south of the equator.

Winds rotate counterclockwise in the Northern Hemisphere.

equator

Winds rotate clockwise in the Southern Hemisphere.

Cloud shapes show the cyclone's whirling wind patterns as Tracy heads straight for Darwin, Australia. (Artist's depiction)

Tornado

SUPER-OUTBREAK, SOUTH & EAST UNITED STATES, 2011

In late April, 2011, a series of ferocious tornadoes tore through the southeast and east of the United States. More than 340 "twisters" were reported over a four-day period, leaving about the same number of people dead.

The 2011 Super-Outbreak was the fourth most deadly series of tornadoes in U.S. history. Alabama bore the brunt of the damage, with over 230 killed. But "twisters" broke out in at least a dozen states, from Texas north and east all the way to New York. The total damage was estimated at $10 billion U.S. in 2011 prices. (Hurricane Katrina's costs, adjusted for 2011 prices, were over ten times more.)

The Super-Outbreak began on April 25. A cyclone or **low** (see page 12) developed over Oklahoma and Missouri. Unusually high temperatures—over 90 degrees Fahrenheit (32 degrees Celsius)—strengthened the wind and rain, and set off many thunderstorms. More big storms joined as the whole system tracked east and north. The next day there were worsening storms and more tornadoes in Louisiana and Arkansas, and outbreaks as far north as the Great Lakes. April 27 saw the fifth greatest one-day death toll for U.S. tornadoes. Just after 5 p.m. an especially massive twister hit Tuscaloosa, Alabama, and raced on to Birmingham. It was around 1.5 miles (2.4 kilometers) wide, had winds of 190 miles per hour (305 kilometers per hour), smashed flat a path 80 miles (130 kilometers) long, and claimed 43 victims.

THE SCIENCE OF TORNADOES

Tornadoes usually form under very large thunderstorms called **supercells** (see page 5). These have spinning winds of cool air inside. Heavy rainfall pulls the spinning winds and their cloud droplets down to the ground in a funnel shape of mist. Warm air near the ground mixes in heat energy to power the winds, which can reach 300 miles per hour (480 kilometers per hour). Usually after an hour this process fades, the tornado narrows like a length of rope, and dies.

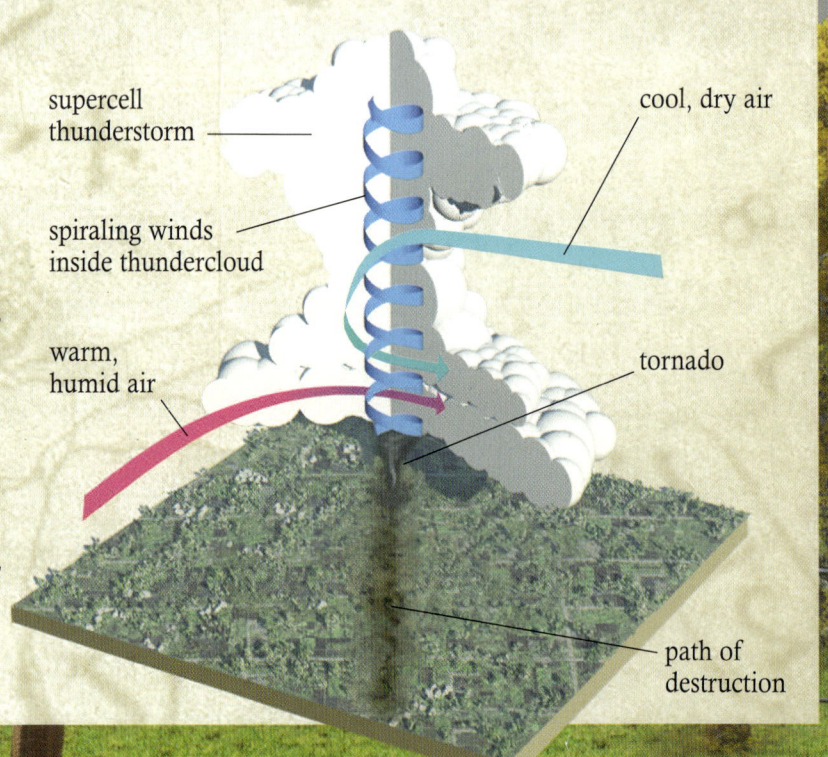

- supercell thunderstorm
- spiraling winds inside thundercloud
- warm, humid air
- cool, dry air
- tornado
- path of destruction

On April 27 more than 50 tornadoes ripped through Alabama, destroying almost everything in their way. (Artist's depiction)

Waterspout
SYDNEY, AUSTRALIA, 2011

A waterspout seems to suck up the surface of a lake or sea, high into the dark cloud above. But this narrow, swirling, funnel-like column rarely lifts up much water. The funnel is caused when water vapor in the swirling air cools and condenses into droplets, as it rises to where air is colder.

There are two main types of waterspouts. The **tornadic** type forms in a similar way to a tornado on land, as explained on the previous page. Swirling winds and mists of water droplets descend from the rotating winds in a huge **supercell** thundercloud. With heat energy and moisture from the water surface, the funnel continues to spin for up to 30 minutes, moving slowly with the parent cloud. The other type, the **fair-weather waterspout**, is shown below.

Waterspouts hardly ever lift surface water, so they do not suck up boats or swimmers. But their fast winds, perhaps 60 miles per hour (100 kilometers per hour), twist and shake anything on the surface. So they can tip over or capsize boats, and trap swimmers in deadly currents. Most waterspouts arise in late summer when the water surface is very warm. In one week in 2003, more than 60 were seen over the Great Lakes of North America. Europe has at least 150 each year. More than 500 yearly are seen around Australia's coasts. In June 2011, a set of especially spectacular waterspouts north of Sydney, Australia, were estimated at 2,000 feet (610 meters) high.

THE SCIENCE OF WATERSPOUTS

Fair-weather waterspouts are usually weaker and shorter-lived than tornadic ones. They form beneath looming, flat-based, fluffy- or lumpy-topped cumulus clouds. A column of warm air, laden with water vapor, rises from the surface, and becomes concentrated into a twisting mist by local gusts of wind blowing around.

dark spot forms

1. As warm, moist air rises, incoming winds grow.
2. The winds rotate faster, creating a circle of spray.
3. The spinning winds rise due to their warmth.
4. A spinning column of water droplets develops.
5. The column reaches to the cloud above.

A giant waterspout over 2,000 feet (610 meters) high menaces the coast of Australia near Sydney. (Artist's depiction)

Superstorm

STORM OF THE CENTURY, EASTERN NORTH AMERICA, 1993

March 12–13, 1993, saw one of the most severe, widespread storm systems in North American history. Almost the entire East Coast suffered freezing temperatures, ferocious winds, and snows that sometimes turned into blizzards. Electricity, communications, and travel took a terrific battering.

The "Storm of the Century" was an especially huge extratropical cyclone (see page 12). Its central area of low pressure started in the Gulf of Mexico, just as a massive **anticyclone** of high pressure settled over the Midwest and Great Plains, with icy air dragged down from the Arctic. Then two sets of high-level winds from the **jet stream** came together to deepen the cyclone's low pressure. Many separate storms built into a giant and headed north from Florida, up the East Coast to Canada.

At the peak of the superstorm, more than half of U.S. states had severe weather. Even normally mild Alabama received 12 inches (30 centimeters) of snow. Florida's derecho winds exceeded 100 miles per hour (160 kilometers per hour). More than 10 tornadoes sprang up. North to New York and beyond, blizzards drifted to 33 feet (10 meters) deep. Roofs collapsed from the snow's weight. Telephone networks were overwhelmed, nearly all transportation shut down, and electricity failed to 10 million people. The final death toll was about 310, stretching almost 2,000 miles (3,219 kilometers) from Cuba all the way north to Newfoundland, Canada.

THE SCIENCE OF DERECHOS

Derechos (see also page 5) are fierce, gusty winds ahead of a thunderstorm or storm complex. As warm air rises over cold air, the region or front between the two develops rolling "tunnels" of winds, like rubbing modeling clay between two palms. These form a squall line which can be hundreds of miles (kilometers) long, with gusts as strong as 200 miles per hour (320 kilometers per hour).

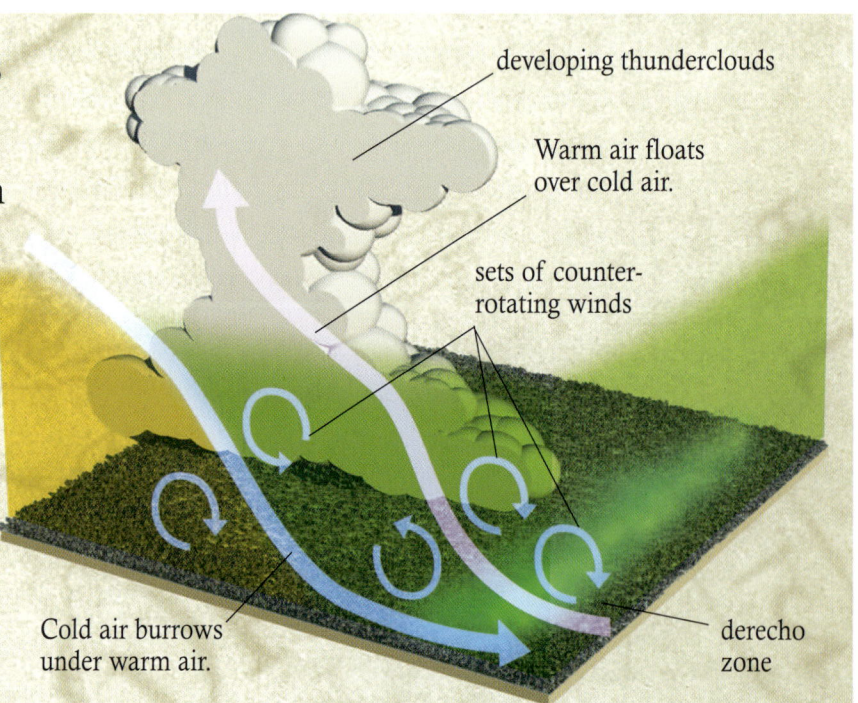

- developing thunderclouds
- Warm air floats over cold air.
- sets of counter-rotating winds
- Cold air burrows under warm air.
- derecho zone

A ship runs into towering waves during the Storm of the Century, and brave helicopter crews race to the rescue. (Artist's depiction)

Blizzard
NORTHWEST-CENTRAL IRAN, 1972

Most northern regions are prepared for heavy snowstorms and even blizzards. Daily life may get disturbed, but not for long. However, when blizzards hit places that rarely have snow, the results can be catastrophic.

Blizzards combine heavy snow with strong winds that cause drifting and a fatal wind-chill factor for anyone caught out in the open. The U.S. Great Blizzard of 1888 affected many northeast states. More than 400 died, including dozens of sailors on ships that were sunk by the winds. As bad as this was, an estimated ten times this number were killed in Southwest Asia, in the Iran Blizzard of 1972. This was the worst blizzard in recorded history for loss of life.

In early February of that year, snow and winds ravaged central Iran. Especially hard-hit were the city of Ardakan, the villages around, and regions to the northwest and south. The chances of such severe weather here are once every 20,000 years. The average snowfall measured up to 10 feet (three meters) but some southern hills had twice this much. It was blown by sweeping winds into drifts that covered whole houses, even entire villages. People in this relatively poor area, with a dry climate and often difficult farming conditions, were well used to hardship. However even they could not endure being trapped in their homes for days, many without heat or enough food. More than 4,000 people perished.

Across central Iran, all road and rail links were closed for more than a week by the blizzard of 1972. (Artist's depiction)

Direction of cold front

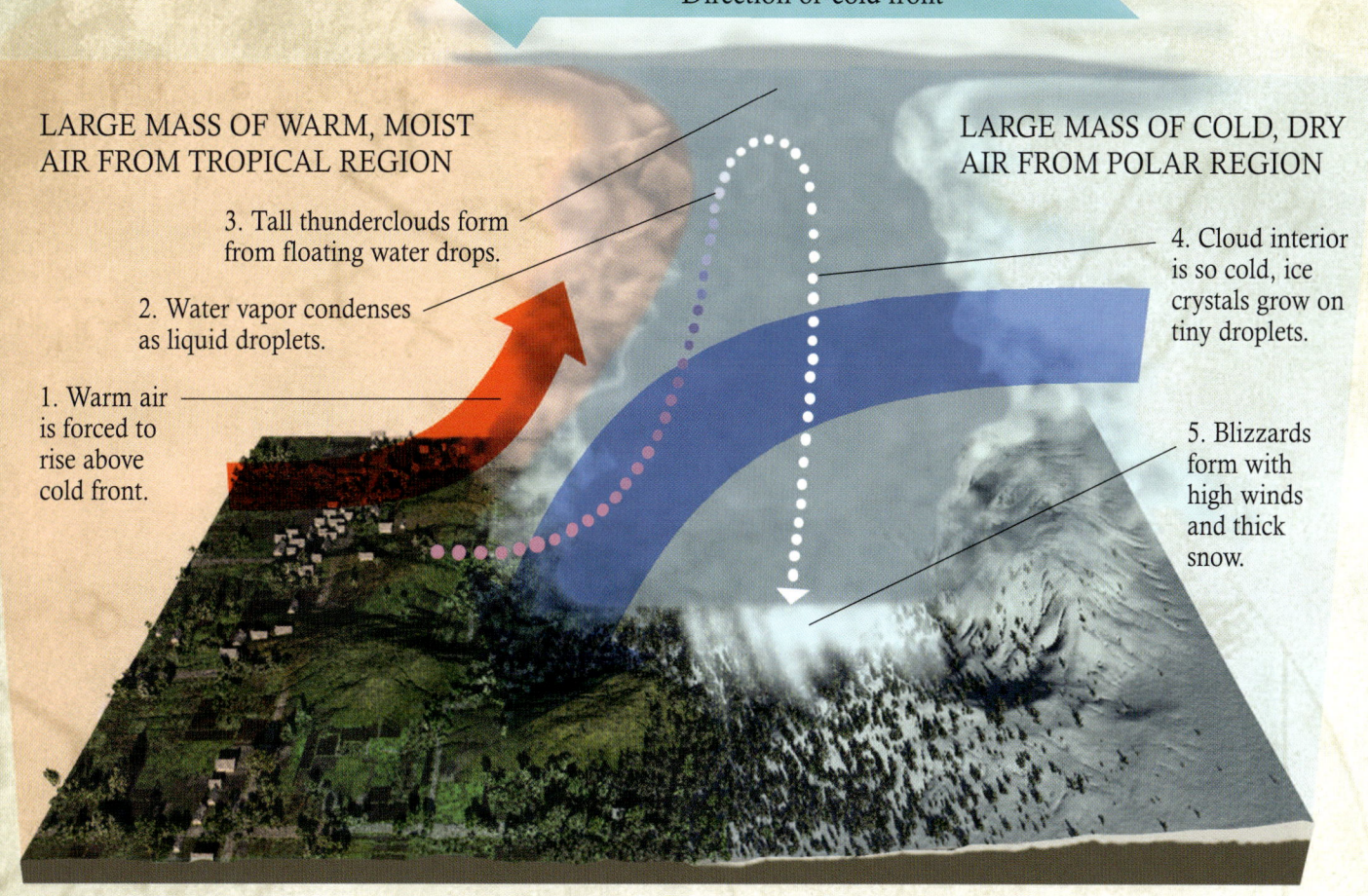

LARGE MASS OF WARM, MOIST AIR FROM TROPICAL REGION

3. Tall thunderclouds form from floating water drops.

2. Water vapor condenses as liquid droplets.

1. Warm air is forced to rise above cold front.

LARGE MASS OF COLD, DRY AIR FROM POLAR REGION

4. Cloud interior is so cold, ice crystals grow on tiny droplets.

5. Blizzards form with high winds and thick snow.

THE SCIENCE OF BLIZZARDS

Snowstorms are similar to extra-cold thunderstorms (see page 5). Water falls, not as liquid, but frozen as six-sided ice crystals called snowflakes, due to the intense cold in the clouds—below minus 30 degrees Fahrenheit (minus 34 degrees Celsius). When does a snowstorm become a blizzard? First, when winds blow faster than 35 miles per hour (56 kilometers per hour). Second, when you can see less than about 440 yards (402 meters) due to the falling or windblown drifting snow. Third, when the whole event lasts a considerable time, usually at least three hours, but often days.

Houses, farms, crops, and livestock drown or wash away in Pakistan's deadly monsoon floods. (Artist's depiction)

Monsoon Flood

PAKISTAN, SOUTH ASIA, 2010

Monsoon rains are not only great weather events, they are a way of life—and death. In 2010, Pakistan suffered the worst monsoons in living memory. One-fifth of the country flooded and almost 2,000 people died.

Monsoons are seasonal heavy rains that fall in many tropical and subtropical regions—especially across South and Southeast Asia. They usually arrive in summer and bring huge amounts of rainfall. From late July 2010, especially heavy monsoon rains began to affect most of Pakistan, especially the hill country to the northwest and west. More than 11 inches (almost 27 centimeters) fell around the city of Peshawar in the far northwest in just 24 hours. The capital, Islamabad, was one of many regions that recorded over 16 inches (40 centimeters) of rain during four days in late July.

As the main monsoon clouds moved south toward the Indian Ocean, smaller rivers fed their torrential downpours into the Indus River, which runs northeast to southwest through the heart of Pakistan. Downstream, floods soon spread to cover more than one-fifth of the whole country. Two million homes were inundated, a quarter of a million cattle and other livestock died, and vast areas of farmland were made useless. About five million people, mostly in small villages, went hungry. By mid-September the floods were mostly gone. But their aftermath is so great, recovery will take at least ten years.

THE SCIENCE OF MONSOONS

Monsoons are like giant versions of the sea breezes familiar around coasts. Land heats up fast in the summer Sun. The air above rises, drawing moisture-laden air from the sea. This also rises and its water vapor condenses to fall as heavy rain. In winter the land cools fast while the sea keeps some heat, so the winds reverse.

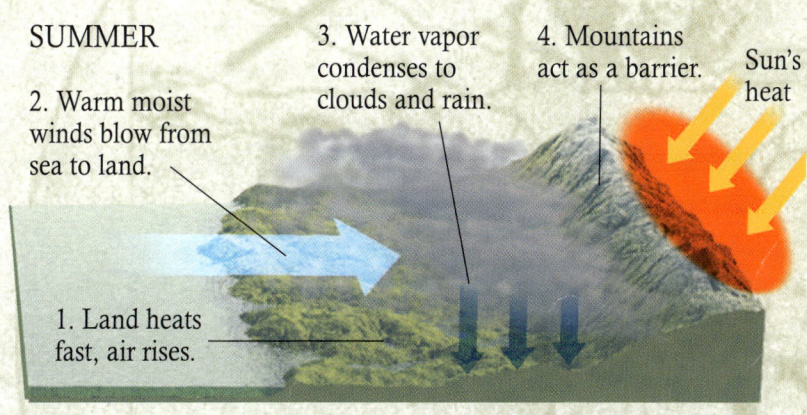

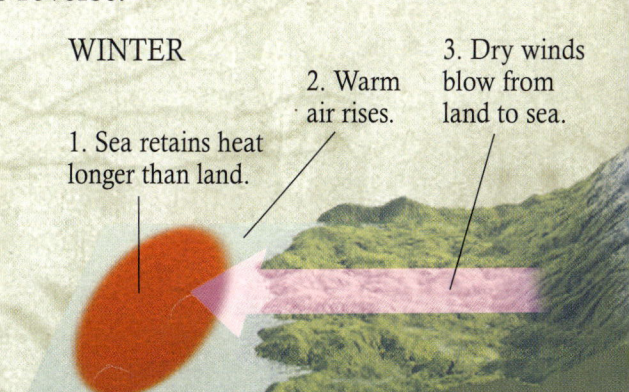

SUMMER
1. Land heats fast, air rises.
2. Warm moist winds blow from sea to land.
3. Water vapor condenses to clouds and rain.
4. Mountains act as a barrier.
Sun's heat

WINTER
1. Sea retains heat longer than land.
2. Warm air rises.
3. Dry winds blow from land to sea.

THE SCIENCE OF DUSTSTORMS AND SANDSTORMS

As a mass of cold, dry air moves over hot ground, its front warms and rises to cause powerful winds blowing along and upward. Small, loose particles of soil, sand, and dust rub and bounce along, knocking bits off each other. They become smaller, lighter, and more likely to get airborne. As this happens, the rubbing or friction generates static electricity. The negatively-charged particles push away or repel the ground. This increases the numbers that get lifted and carried along by the swirling air currents.

Tumbling grains collide and break into smaller fragments light enough to blow into the air.

2. Strong winds form from local storms or cold fronts.

3. Sand grains stay low.

1. Ground is very dry and loose.

4. Dust particles are lifted very high.

Baghdad becomes a dusty ghost town during the week-long sandstorm. (Artist's depiction)

Sandstorm

NORTHWEST IRAQ, 2009

Winds that swirl around dust and sand are a common hazard in dry regions. But when such winds last a week, as in Iraq in 2009, they cause problems varying from breathing difficulties to transport shutdown.

Small, short-lived sand- and duststorms often occur around large thunderstorms—including those without rain. But the Great Duststorm in Iraq in early July 2009, was due largely to a series of cold fronts (as explained opposite). The storm was so bad because the land was exceptionally dry, for three main reasons. One, the chief rivers of the region, Euphrates and Tigris, were much reduced due to dams and water taken for crops upstream. Their waters could not soak and spread into the land. Two, there had been several years of drought. Three, poor farming methods stripped the soil of stabilizing plant roots and nourishment.

Dust and sand covered everything outside. The strong winds forced particles around windows and doors into rooms, coating everything here, too. Visibility was so poor that in Iraq's capital, Baghdad, many planes, trains, and buses were cancelled. With no clean air, day after day, people flocked to hospitals with serious breathing problems.

Heatwave

WESTERN EUROPE, 2003

In mid-July 2003, Western Europe was enjoying summer warmth and Sun. One month later, it was in the stifling grip of a severe heatwave with water shortages, electricity outages, crop failures, and 40,000-plus deaths.

Fine weather in summer varies from a few days to a week, perhaps two. A heatwave is considerably longer—usually three weeks or more. There is no exact temperature to mark the event, only that it should be several degrees above normal for the area, and for an unusually long period. There were signs of Western Europe's building 2003 heatwave as early as June. A region of high pressure developed with calm, clear skies. This grew so large that, coupled with the abnormal position of the jet stream, it blocked other smaller, cooler weather systems trying to disturb it.

France was hit hardest, with almost 15,000 deaths due to excessive heat. These were mostly elderly people, who were already weak, and perhaps suffering from breathing problems in the stale, polluted air. As air-conditioning, refrigerators, and deep-freezers worked harder, electricity supplies strained to breaking point. Thirsty crops withered under the glaring Sun. Grapes for wine, and wheat for bread and pasta, had poor harvests. Nature suffered too as wildfires broke out, and fish and other water creatures perished in drying lakes and rivers.

A Spanish farmer checks a calf overcome by heat exhaustion during the European heatwave. (Artist's depiction)

The Science of Heatwaves

Often a major heatwave combines an unusually large mass of hot air with an unusual position of the jet stream. The two work together to block off other weather systems. Lack of hills and other land features mean the heating is relatively even, which reduces any chance of winds. As the ground and air warm undisturbed, skies stay clear. Gradually dust and fumes build up in the hot, stale, static atmosphere.

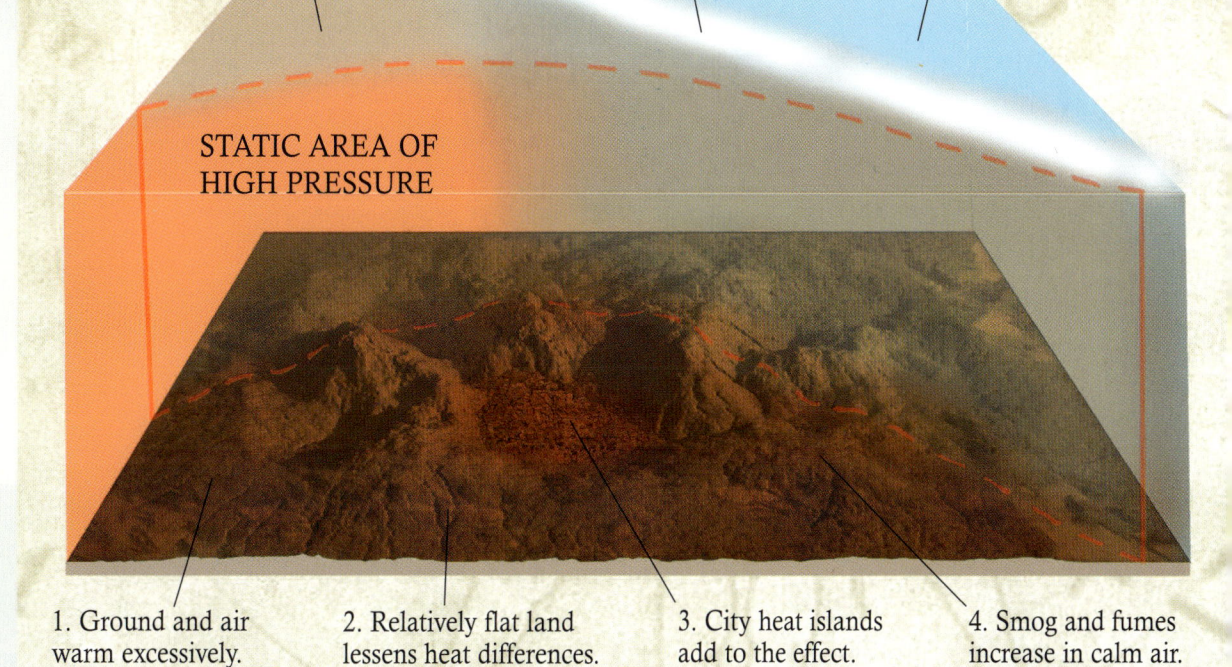

7. Cloudless skies allow yet more of the Sun's heat to reach the surface.

6. Jet stream keeps weather systems separate.

5. Cool air tries to move in and change the weather.

STATIC AREA OF HIGH PRESSURE

1. Ground and air warm excessively.

2. Relatively flat land lessens heat differences.

3. City heat islands add to the effect.

4. Smog and fumes increase in calm air.

THE SCIENCE OF LIGHTNING

Rising warm air in parts of a thunderstorm lift water droplets so high, they freeze into ice particles. These fall, create downdrafts of air, and rub against rising drops. Rubbing or friction causes static electricity—positive for ice near the cloud top, and negative for water drops below. The electricity builds until it jumps as a massive spark or lightning bolt, thousands of yards (meters) long. We see bolts within a cloud as flickers of sheet lightning. Between the cloud and the ground we see branched paths of forked lightning.

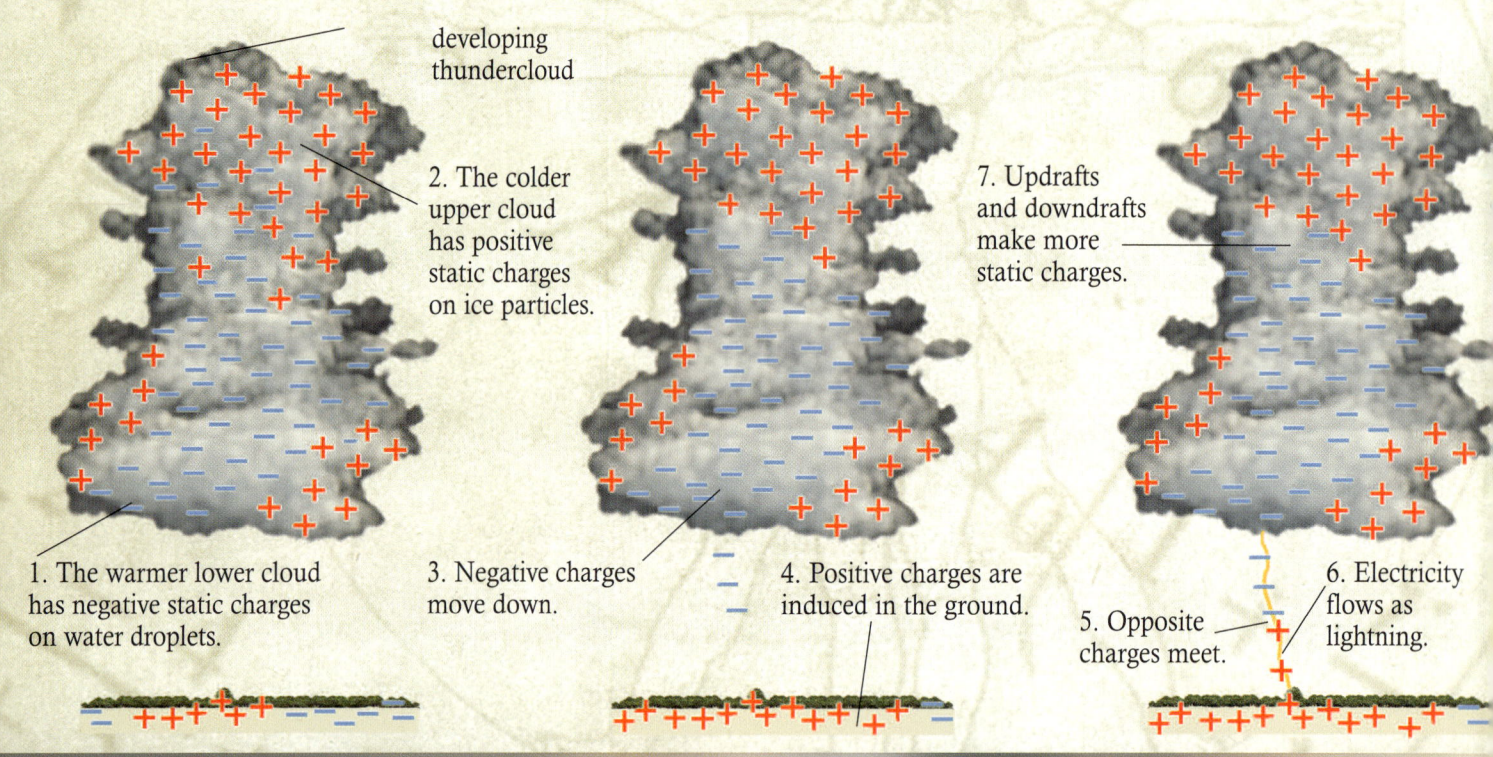

developing thundercloud

1. The warmer lower cloud has negative static charges on water droplets.

2. The colder upper cloud has positive static charges on ice particles.

3. Negative charges move down.

4. Positive charges are induced in the ground.

5. Opposite charges meet.

6. Electricity flows as lightning.

7. Updrafts and downdrafts make more static charges.

High winds fan flames toward a ranch during the Black Saturday outbreak. (Artist's depiction)

Lightning and Wildfire

BLACK SATURDAY, VICTORIA STATE, AUSTRALIA, 2009

February 7, 2009, was a black day in Australian history. After a long, hot, dry spell, hundreds of bushfires sprang up in the southeast state of Victoria. The eventual death toll was 173, with over 5,000 injured.

Lightning is the main natural "spark" that sets off wildfires. The land is generally dry after warm weather, so the flames catch easily. Less common causes are red-hot lava and hot ash from a volcanic eruption, also rockfalls that spark, as when flint rocks are struck. Natural clear rock crystals may even focus the Sun's rays like a magnifier lens into a hotspot.

But human triggers for wildfires are all too common. Electricity lines fall or spark. Camp fires, barbecues, or cigarettes are carelessly left. Power tools throw out sparks. Winds fan controlled burns, such as clearing forest for crops or grazing animals. And there are fires started deliberately, as criminal acts.

Australia's Black Saturday was named after the toll of deaths and injuries, and also the blackened landscapes left by the merciless flames. A two-month heatwave, up to 120 degrees Fahrenheit (49 degrees Celsius), had left the land tinder-dry. Changeable winds of 75 miles per hour (120 kilometers per hour) made the flames race through the bush faster than anyone could even drive. More than 2,000 houses were totally destroyed and almost 8,000 people became homeless. The terrible tragedy was worsened by police work that showed some fires were arson—started on purpose. Australia's Prime Minister called it "mass murder."

Disasters World Map

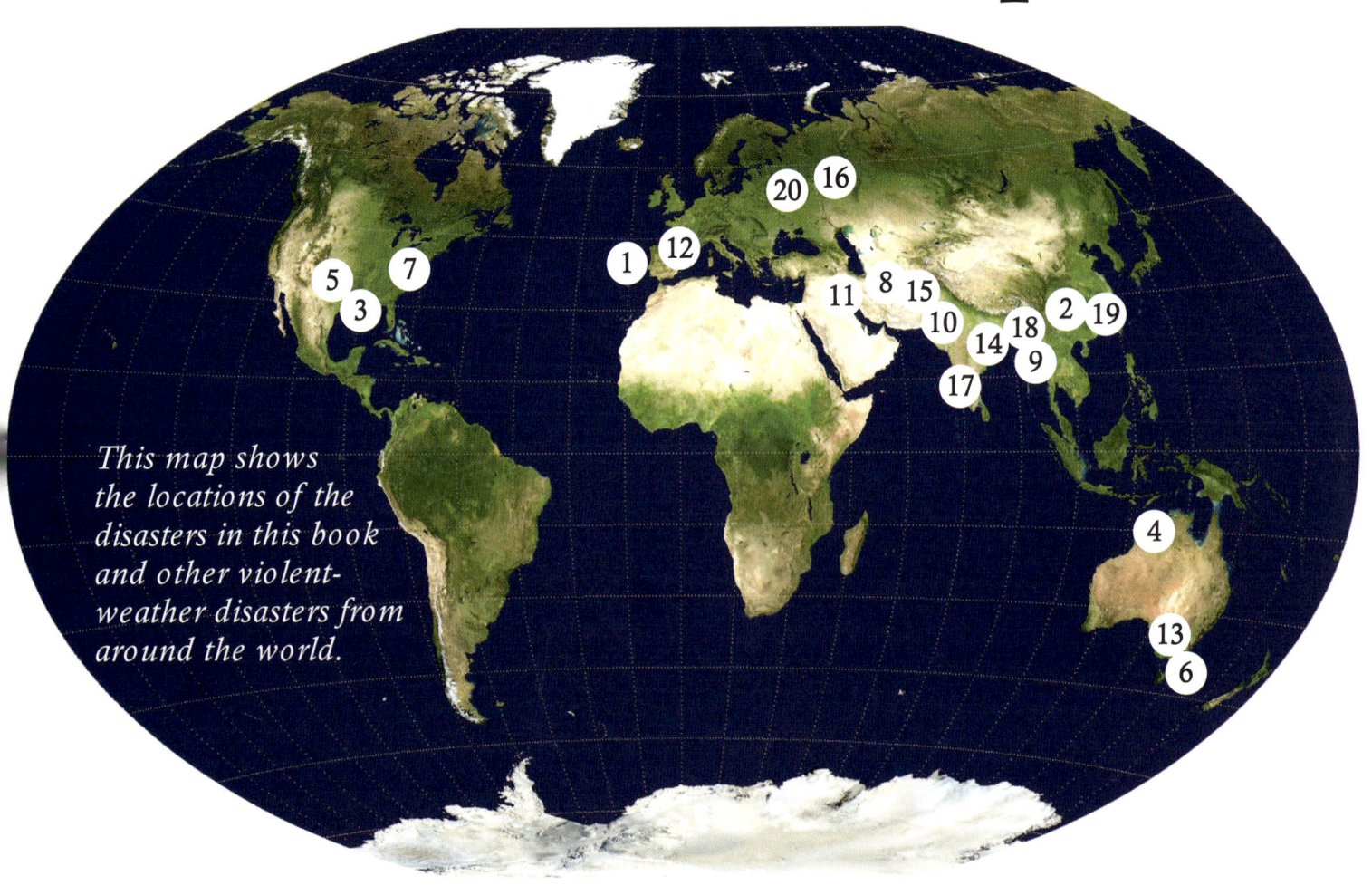

This map shows the locations of the disasters in this book and other violent-weather disasters from around the world.

1. Martinair Flight 495 Microburst, Faro, Portugal, 1992
2. Guizhou Hailstorms, South China, 2011
3. Hurricane Katrina, United States, 2005
4. Cyclone Tracy, Northern Australia, 1974
5. Tornado Super-Outbreak, South & East United States, 2011
6. Waterspout, Sydney, Australia, 2011
7. Storm of the Century, Eastern North America, 1996
8. Iran Blizzard, 1972
9. Cyclone Nargis, Myanmar (Burma), 2008
10. Pakistan Monsoon Floods, 2010
11. Iraq Sandstorm, 2009
12. Western Europe Heatwave, 2003
13. Black Saturday Bushfires, Victoria State, Australia, 2009
14. Bangladesh Cyclone, 1991
15. Afghanistan Blizzard, 2008
16. Russian Heatwave, 2010
17. Southern India heatwave, 2003
18. Daulatpur-Salturia Tornado, Manikganj, Bangladesh, 1989
19. Black Dragon Fire, China, 1987
20. Ivanovo-Yaroslavl Tornado, Russia, 1984

30

Glossary

anticyclone A rotating system of winds spiraling around an area of high pressure. Anticyclones turn the opposite way to cyclones—clockwise to the north of the equator, counterclockwise to the south.

condense When a gas or vapor turns into a liquid, which also gives out energy in the form of heat, and so warms the surroundings

Coriolis Effect The angled or twisting deflection given to moving objects due to the daily rotation of Earth

cumulonimbus A tall or towering cloud with a white or pale upper part, often flat-topped like an anvil, and a dark base which releases rain, hail, or snow. This is the typical thundercloud.

depression An area of depressed or low air or atmospheric pressure, also called a "low"

derecho Strong, gusting winds that move ahead of, or to the sides of, thunderstorms or similar large storms or showers

evaporate When a liquid turns into a gas or vapor, which also takes in energy in the form of heat, and so cools the surroundings

extratropical cyclone A rotating or spinning system of winds, clouds, and rain, spiraling inward to an area of low pressure, that occurs away from tropical regions

fair-weather waterspout A waterspout that forms low near the water's surface, usually below cumulus clouds, and extends upward to reach the clouds

jet stream Narrow, fast, high-level winds that flow in regular patterns, usually where air ceases to cool with height, 4–10 miles (7–16 kilometers)

low An area of depressed or low air or atmospheric pressure, also called a depression

supercell A thunderstorm, usually very large, that has twisting or rotating winds called a mesocyclone inside it. The winds usually blow upward but may reverse and blow down under certain conditions.

tornadic waterspout A waterspout that forms in a similar way to a tornado on land, by a twisting column of water descending from a cloud (usually a thundercloud)

tropical cyclone A rotating system of winds, spiraling inward to an area of low pressure, that occurs in tropical regions. Examples of powerful tropical cyclones with heavy rain and strong winds are hurricanes, typhoons, and the storms simply called "cyclones."

Index

A
anticyclone 18
Australia 12, 13, 16, 17, 29
B
blizzards 18, 20–21
C
cold fronts 21, 24
Coriolis Effect 12, 13
cyclones 10, 12–13, 14, 18
D
derecho winds 5, 18
duststorms 24, 25
E
electricity 5, 18, 24, 26, 28, 29
extratropical cyclones 12, 18
F
fair-weather waterspout 16
Faro, Portugal 6–7
floods 11, 23
G
Guizhou Province, China 8–9
H
hail 5, 6, 8, 9, 11
hailstorm 8–9
heatwave 26–27, 29
hurricanes 10–11, 12, 14

I
ice 5, 8, 9, 21, 28
Iran Blizzard 20–21
Iraq Duststorm 24–25
J
jet stream 18, 26, 27
L
lightning 4, 5, 28–29
M
Martinair Flight 495 6–7
microburst 5, 6–7
monsoon flood 22–23
P
Pakistan, South Asia 22–23
polluted air 26
R
rain, rainstorms 5, 6, 11, 12, 14, 23, 25
S
sandstorm 24–25
snow 18, 20, 21
snowstorms 20, 21
Storm of the Century 18–19
superstorms 18–19

T
thunderclouds 4, 5, 28
 blizzards 21
 hailstorms 8, 9
 microbursts 6
 superstorms 18
 waterspouts 16
thunderstorm 4–5, 11, 14, 18, 28
 hailstorms 8
 superstorms 18
 tornadoes 6, 14
tornadic waterspout 16
tornadoes 5, 6, 14–15, 18
twisters 5, 6, 14
typhoons 10, 12
U
United States 10–11, 14, 18, 20
W
waterspout 16–17
Western Europe 26–27
wildfire 28–29
winds
 blizzards 20, 21
 cyclones 10, 11, 12, 13
 monsoon floods 23
 sandstorms 24, 25
 superstorms 18
 thunderstorms 5, 6
 tornadoes 14
 waterspouts 16
 wildfires 28, 29